# Fiat Ordo

**A GUIDE FOR FAITHFUL MOMS**

**WITH BUSY LIVES**

**ELAYNE MILLER**

Fiat Ordo: A Guide for Faithful Moms with Busy Lives by Elayne Miller

Published by Annunciation Designs, LLC

PO Box 180, Alpha, OH 45301-0180

www.annunciationdesigns.com

© 2018 Elayne miller

All rights reserved. No portion of this book may be reproduced in any form without permission from the publisher, except as permitted by U.S. copyright law. For permissions contact:

annunciationdesigns@gmail.com

For bulk orders or wholesale orders, contact:
annunciationdesigns@gmail.com

Cover by Elayne Miller

ISBN: 978-1724820341

For Dominic and Benedict

∞

# Introduction

FIAT ORDO

*- Let there be order -*

Let's begin with a prayer.

"*Lord, fiat ordo. Bring order into my heart and into my life. Give me the strength to cling to order when chaos swirls around me. Give me the humility to remain ordered to you when temptations abound. Give me the patience to sit in ordered silence rather than fill the emptiness with noise. Let there be order.*"

Friend, as we begin this journey, I thought it would be helpful to tell you a little about myself. I am roughly 30 years old, with a faithful husband and a sweet toddler. I studied engineering, worked as a high-school math teacher for four years, and now stay home with my son, teach math online, and run a small business. The summer my son was born, I was finishing a degree, starting a business, and preparing three courses for the upcoming school year. I have been so busy and so stressed that I've had panic attacks. I have worked long into the night to prepare for class the next day and spent hours perfecting assessments and lecture slides. I have spent nearly every nap-time for the last two years designing, fulfilling orders, creating PowerPoints, sewing, grading, and occasionally napping myself. When I write that it is possible to have order in your life, I mean order amidst the chaos. I love being busy. I love working until I'm exhausted. However, I know that I am a better mother, wife, teacher, and friend when the busyness of my life is properly ordered. That, my friend, is what I'd like to help you work toward as well.

When I describe this book to acquaintances, I typically get one reaction. "So, you've really got this figured out, huh." I'd like to clarify right up front that I in no way have this all figured out. Most of my motivation in writing this book is that I personally need this book. I need a guide to help me see the good, true, and beautiful in my life and stay ordered even when every book, block, and truck is off the shelf.

As I designed the cover of this book, I was reflecting on order in chaos. My hand-lettering business is based on the principle of helping families call to mind the Sacred in the midst of the ordinary. Truly, my goal with this guide is the same. And so, my thoughts journeyed to my beekeeper husband's hives. They literally buzz with activity all day, bees flying in and out and communicating, and baby bees being hatched and raised, and honey being stored. Despite all this busyness, the bee is a symbol of orderly perfection. Busy yet ordered was the perfect imagery. Additionally, the bee is a symbol for Our Lady, which was important to me personally.

This journey is meant to be completed one day at a time. Don't try to rush! Change takes time; conversion takes reflection. Completed one day at a time, I hope that this journey will have lasting benefits in your life. It may not make your to-do list shorter, but I hope that it can help you acquire some skills to calm your soul and prioritize the tasks before you.

A few ground rules:

1) Believe in yourself! You are capable of making changes to improve your physical, spiritual, and mental health! This may take time. You may make some changes as you journey through this book the first time, and then find yourself ready to tackle other areas later.
2) Please, actually write down your responses to the various prompts. The act of writing helps improve memory, and seeing your thoughts written out will encourage you to make the changes necessary.
3) At the beginning of each reflection is a short prayer, formatted in a script font. Stop and offer a heartfelt prayer with those words.

Let's begin!

# Day 1

*Lord, give me clarity.*

I believe that, in any journey, we must first determine where we begin. Today I'd like you to take stock of your life. On any given day, what are your feelings about the life you've built? Do you feel worn down, as though you're falling further and further behind? Do you long for 'one day' when you'll have a chance to clean the fridge and catch up on laundry? Have you simply decided that this is how your life will be – no use fighting it?

As a teacher, I work long hours. My husband has never quite been able to understand the work I put in. I used to work as an engineer too, so I know where he's coming from – you do the work, you go home. But it's different for teachers, for small business owners, and for all those who work from home. You don't get to 'leave the office,' because the office is at home. You probably care deeply about the work you do, and it is a part of you. It's never far from your mind, your heart. This is the beautiful part of working from home, but it also presents so many challenges.

When I was retiring to the couch for two hours of work every evening after my son fell asleep, begging my supportive husband for more time to work every weekend, and trying to finish a large batch of products on Sunday morning before breakfast with my parents, we realized I had a problem. I was not properly prioritizing my family. My life was not properly ordered.

My vocation is first to be a wife and a mother. My role is to help my family get to Heaven. How has your primary vocation taken a backseat to your work?

*Describe your <u>feelings</u> about the state of your life. Do you feel balanced? Do you have time for yourself and undivided* *attention to give your children and husband? Are you feeling overwhelmed or perhaps underwhelmed with your life? Have you found more joy than you could ever describe? Is this motherhood thing just different from what you expected?*

# Day 2

*Lord, open my eyes.*

Yesterday, you wrote down your feelings about your current life. Today, we're going to continue to explore the areas that you would like to work on throughout this journey. The first step is identifying the problems!

I saw that for my family, quality time meant something different for each of us. I was happy simply being in the same room as my husband, while I worked on prepping classes and he had time to unwind after work. My husband did not view this as 'time spent together.' My son, even before he could walk, would close my laptop if I attempted to squeeze in work. He instinctively felt that my attention should not be given to technology rather than the life in front of me. My family was teaching me, but it took me a long time to listen.

Think through your days. Be as specific as you can as you list the things you would like to improve in your daily life. Some areas that may come to mind:

- Prayer time
- Personal time
- Time with your husband
- Joyful (non-stressed) time with children
- Less clutter
- Business/work time
- Space for working
- Need for help around the house
- Financial peace

I'm sure you also have your own unique challenges!

*What areas of my life would I like to see improved?*

# Day 3

*Lord, thank you for the blessings you have given me.*

I want to encourage you to recognize and give thanks for the joys in your life! I asked you to identify challenge areas first, in order to clear them out of your mind and allow you to focus on the good. Put aside the list of challenges and think only about the parts of your life that give you joy.

When I take time to reflect, I find so much about my life that brings me joy. Too soon after my son was born, I returned to work for a year of teaching. I will not take my current ability to work from home for granted! It is hard, but it is exactly where I am meant to be. I love my online teaching job and give thanks for the women with whom I work. They have made my transition to the digital classroom mostly seamless. I am continually blown away by supporters of my small business and love creating, designing, and interacting with customers.

My life is so filled with joy, but I sometimes manage to overlook that when I am straining to complete work under a deadline, late in grading student papers, or staring at a living room covered in blocks. That's the reason this practice of gratitude is incredibly important. I encourage you, beyond this one day in this journey, to begin a gratitude journal as a habit. It's amazing how much simply bringing those wonderful parts of your life to the forefront can impact your general happiness.


*For what are you grateful? What parts of your life bring you joy?*

# Day 4

*Lord, you place these desires on my heart. Grant me the grace to bring them to life.*

Now that we have spent a few days analyzing the current status of your life, let's day dream a little. If you had a dream about a perfect, regular day, what would it look like? Try to keep your dream within the confines of your actual life – as in, the setting is the town in which you currently reside, all your children are around, your husband still works (if that is real-life for you). Daydream about a lovely, normal day. What would you 'accomplish?' How would you feel?

As an example, I'll describe my perfect normal day. I wake up at 7:00 refreshed after 8 hours of sleep. I eat breakfast in quiet (my husband already at work, toddler asleep) and then work on business tasks on my computer. My son wakes up at 8:00 and I change him and feed him breakfast. We find something fun for my son to do – visit a library, park, or museum, or play in the backyard. We eat a healthy lunch I packed, then head home. I tidy the house and spend a few minutes preparing for supper while my son plays or 'helps.' Around 1:00, I rock my son and he settles into his crib to sleep for two hours. Meanwhile, I work on teaching or business tasks. When he awakes, I play with him while preparing a healthy supper. My husband arrives home from work and we sit down together for supper at 5:00. We clean up together, then spend time as a family. We might go on a walk, play in the backyard, or play a game in the living room. At 7:30, we do bedtime routine, my son falls asleep, and I spend an hour with my husband. After he goes to sleep, I work for 1-2 hours and then shower and fall asleep.

I want to remind you that I'm not saying every (or any) day at my house looks like this. I am saying this is my dream!

*What does your dream day look like?*

# Day 5

*Lord, give me the grace to meet the demands of my vocation.*

We have had a chance to daydream. Next, we will begin to reconcile our dreams with the reality of our vocation. What responsibilities do you have on a daily or weekly basis? This includes your work, household, children, husband, faith, and importantly, yourself.

Work tasks are usually easy to define. Knowing exactly what your children and husband require from you can take a lot of searching and trial-and-error. Knowing what you, yourself, need can be daunting. My husband has helped me immensely by recognizing, even before I have, when I need a quiet break. I feel so guilty about interrupting family time to sit in a dark room for ten minutes, but as a busy introvert, it's a necessity.

*List your responsibilities below*

Work (including required times, tasks, etc)

_____

_____

_____

_____

_____

_____

Household (including various chores, cooking, cleaning, etc)

_____

Children and husband (sports practice, homeschool, etc)

Faith life, personal, other (alone time, Adoration, Scripture study, etc)

# Day 6

*Lord, help me to fulfill my responsibilities joyfully.*

It's time to take the first step toward making your dream day a reality. Take some time to read over your dream day and your responsibilities. What needs to be added to your dream day to make it more practical? What needs to be subtracted?

For my family, an hour of quiet work in the morning is not practical. My son wakes up before 7:30 more often than not. This typically leaves me with a few minutes to eat breakfast and read a devotional, and then my son is awake. I have learned not to leave anything time sensitive for the morning. If he happens to sleep, I work ahead on something. If he wakes up, I'm not starting my day on a bad foot, wishing I had just a little more time to myself. I can throw myself into mothering joyfully.

*What differences do you notice between your dream day and your responsibilities? What parts of your dream day are simply not practical given your current state of life? What parts of your responsibilities could be molded to fit more neatly with your ideal day?*

EVERY ONE OF US NEEDS *half an hour of prayer* EVERY DAY, EXCEPT *when we are busy* — THEN WE NEED *an hour*.

ATTRIBUTED TO
ST. FRANCIS DE SALES

# Day 7

*Saint Zélie, pray for me.*

Saint Zélie Martin is perhaps best known as the mother of the Little Flower, Saint Thérése of Lisieux. She and her saintly husband, Louis Martin, had nine children together, with only five daughters surviving infancy. Zélie worked as a lacemaker; she understood the struggles of working and raising faithful children. In a letter, she wrote, "I'm having all [the girls'] dresses repaired, so I am up to my neck in dressmakers. And in addition to this, I have urgent orders due this week; none are completed, and that worries me." This is a saint for us! She understood the chaos of having five young children, of attempting to work and train and love out of limited energy.

We'll return to this story at the end of our journey, but I wanted to bring Saint Zélie to your attention now. Allow her to be your heavenly guide on the path toward sainthood.

As our final journal entry this week, reflect once more on the life you currently lead, the life you wish to lead, and the life that will move you closer to God and to Heaven.

# Day 8

*Lord, help me rest in you.*

The first week of this journey was about evaluating your current and ideal schedule. Now, we'll take steps toward orienting yourself and your family to your shared goals. We want to start by discussing the idea of control.

As work-from-home moms, I think it can be easy to forget the control we have over our lives. Yes, our children place incredible demands upon us! Think for a moment of the typical office worker – their boss tells them what they will be paid, when they will be at work, how long they have for lunch, and perhaps even what projects to work on at a given time. In contrast, we have the ability to decide when to wake up, when to eat lunch, when to rest and when to power through work. I know, you may be thinking, 'No, actually my kids decide all of that for me." The truth is we *could* wake up earlier – it may be the best decision *not* to, due to lack of sleep, but we have the ability to decide.

The ability to control our days is one of the great benefits of working from home. If you are feeling 'stuck', mired in the muck of day to day life, take time today to reflect on the beauty of this opportunity.

*Why is it that you work from home? Are your reasons financial? Do you want to be the primary caretaker of your children? Do you want ample time with your children to raise them in the faith? Do you have medical reasons? Do you simply have a passion that you wish to share? What advantages does this choice (to work from home, in whatever capacity) offer to you?*

---

---

---

# Day 9

*Lord, help me to see Your plans for me.*

At this point, we want to look seriously at what we can control and what we can't. This is an important step toward reordering our lives. I think it's important to realize just how much we actually do have control over. Many of our actions might feel out of our control only because we do not want the alternative. For instance, my husband's choice of job is within our control. If he chose to find a different job, it might mean major changes for our family for which we are not prepared, but we could choose that change.

For today, think seriously about what you have 'immediate' control over. That is, what could you change in the next day or week? For me, this might include my going to bed earlier, avoiding sugar, and giving my child time with my undivided attention throughout the day. I do not have immediate control over the house I live in or my husband's work schedule. Long term, I can change those things, but for now we'll focus on immediate changes.

*Fill in the following diagram, sorting the decisions in your life that you have full control over, have limited control over, and do not have immediate control over.*

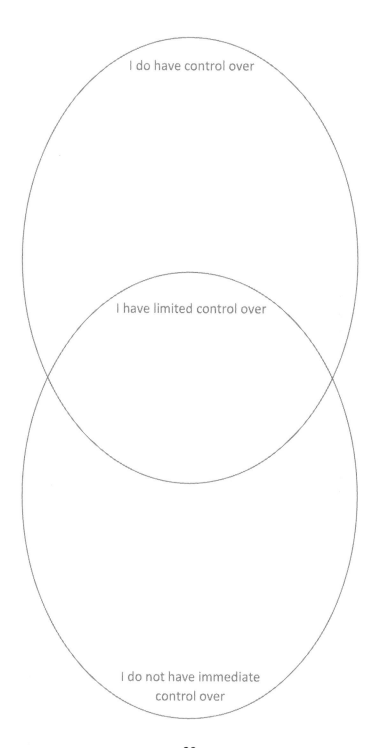

## Day 10

*Lord, help me turn toward you with my thoughts, words, and actions.*

You now have a list of areas of your life over which you have control. Focus on this section and consider what might happen if you press for positive change. How would your day be different? How might you get your children involved? How might your work need to change to fit the needs of your family? Take time with each item you listed that you do have control over, and ponder these questions. Allow yourself to daydream (realistically) about what might happen.

I first completed this exercise a year and a half ago. I saw that my frustration with spending nap times running around the house cleaning was something I could control. I began to clean while my son was playing or crawling after me. It took longer, a lot longer, but when he napped I had uninterrupted time to create. I had told myself that I couldn't clean while he was awake because he complained and I split my attention between sweeping and picking him up. When I attempted a change, great things happened. My son learned about chores, saw me working hard for our family, and learned quickly to play independently. With this success, I attempted at times to work on my computer while he played – which did not go well! He was jealous my attention was on the computer, he tried to type, and he would shut my computer saying, 'All done, Mama!'. God spoke truth into my day through my son.

*What could happen if you allow yourself to change the things you can control?*

# Day 11

*Lord, show me your mission for my family.*

Now that we have begun to focus on your goals, we will spend a few days writing a family mission statement.

Mission statements have long been standard practice in business. When you start a company, the very first steps you are advised to take are to identify your audience and your mission. At one time, I worked as a project engineer for a company that made plastic automotive parts. While there, we had a major accreditation review. Every employee of the company had to either memorize the mission of the company or carry it on a card on their person at all times. I was interviewed by the accreditation team and asked to repeat it. That experience stuck with me, not just because I was new, and terrified I'd be the reason the whole company failed the review, but also because it helped to instill in me the importance of a mission. That company strived to involve us in its mission, to focus all our energies into the ultimate goals of the company.

Sadly, this view of the 'big picture' is not carried into the average family's life, but perhaps it should be.

Let me give you a few reasons why writing a family mission statement might be useful:

- Your family is unique, with its own challenges, strengths, focus, goals, and traditions.
- You desire for your family to live intentionally. Daily life can be taxing, and sometimes we get bogged down in the weeds. We forget to pop our head up once in a while and take stock of where we are and where we want to be headed. When we say we want to live 'intentionally', we mean we want to keep the big goals for our family in mind in all our little decisions.

- Your family desires direction. Without a concise direction, we may not drift where we would hope to go.
- Your family has a goal – to work toward Heaven. A family mission statement is one tool to ensure that all that your family does works *ad majorem Dei gloriam* – toward the greater glory of God.

Spend time brainstorming about what you might include in your family mission statement. It's a great idea to discuss this with your husband and any older children.

# Day 12

*Lord, give me words that will lead us to You.*

Together with your husband, work to define your mission. Discuss particular family values that you most wish to see yourselves and your children live out. Perhaps there are particular saints of devotions that are near to your hearts. How do you dream of your children interacting with each other and with others in the world?

Keep in mind as you write that the goal is not a rulebook for the family, but a statement of mission (rules may flow from the mission, but the mission should be positive and uplifting, not proscriptive).

Decide on the scope of your family mission statement – is there another aspect of life that you would like to include in your mission? Examples include homeschool, a homestead, or a family business. The family mission statement should be general enough that it can last throughout the years.

As you write a rough draft of your family mission statement, I have a few ideas to help:

- The best written family mission statements I have seen have been between 25 and 55 words
- Consider focusing on a quote (from a Saint, Scripture, or the *Catechism of the Catholic Church*) that is central to your beliefs
- Consider the style that fits your family – bullet points, two or three sentences, a motto and a few explanatory phrases, a simple mind-map.

See a few examples on the following pages to help you begin.

*This family loves:*

THE *good*. THE *true*. THE *and* *beautiful*:

LEARNING FOR *discovery's* SAKE:

FOLLOWING *Christ* *and* HIS *Church*:

BEING *present*. *together*. *and* *forgiving*

THE _____ FAMILY

A *God* centered *loving* FAMILY

PATIENTLY *formed* BY *God*

ACTIVELY *love* AND *serve* OTHERS

DO NOT PREACH GREAT THINGS; *live them*

EST. _____

THE _____ FAMILY

TO *cultivate comfort, courage, and compassion* IN OUR *home* AND IN OUR WHOLE HUMAN *family.*

In the _____ family,
we
LOVE God
TELL THE truth
KEEP OUR word
pray EVERYDAY
help OTHERS
MAKE sacrifices
PRACTICE forgiveness
CHOOSE joy
remember WHO WE ARE

**Day 13**

*Lord, speak Your words into my heart.*

Today we are ready to refine the statement.

Read over the entire statement slowly. Ask yourself the following questions:

- Does this statement accurately convey our family's raison d'être, or fundamental reason for existence?
- Is this statement broad enough to apply to all areas of family life?
- From reading this statement, would a stranger have a good idea of the following?
  - Family priorities
  - Family values
  - The elements that make your family unique
  - Are there elements that seem repetitious, out of place, or simply don't sound like your family?

Now you have a starting place for revisions. Be honest about what can be cut out – your family mission is not a place for 'fluff.' A strong and concise statement will be the most useful to your family.

Once you have completed writing your family missions statement, I highly recommend that you display it proudly in your home.

# Day 14

*Pope Saint John Paul II, help me to imitate you.*

One of my favorite Saints is Pope Saint John Paul II. There is so much to be said about his entire life, and if you don't know much about him, I highly recommend his story to you. I would start with *Saint John Paul the Great: His Five Loves* by Jason Evert. Today, I want to focus on something I have heard from people in my life who had the great honor of meeting this saint.

My husband and I were married by a tiny 95-year-old Polish priest. He was granted a group audience with the Pope during a pilgrimage to Rome. Father Bonifas was nervous, and when it was his turn to speak to the Pope, he said the first thing that came to mind, "Thank you for Saint Faustina!!" (As a fellow Pole, Pope John Paul II worked to bring Saint Faustina's message of Christ's Divine Mercy to the world.

Father Bonifas told us that in those short moments, the busy, tired Holy Father fixed him with intense eyes and smiled. Father Bonifas knew that the room was full of fellow priests, but Pope John Paul II gave each person his entire attention. This is someone who read books during meetings, not because he was bored but because he had the mental capacity to do both at once. He could have locked himself in his immense intellect, but instead he focused his entire attention on the person right in front of him. Since hearing Father Bonifas' story, and similar stories from others, I have made this my goal. I want to be so present with the people right in front of me that I'm remembered for it. I have a massive amount of work in front of me in this area, but Pope Saint John Paul inspires me to greatness.

*Does this story resonate with you? Or is there another Saint that you particularly admire? Ask for their intercession and list below how you can work toward sainthood in this way.*

# Day 15

*Lord, give order to my days, that my thoughts have freedom to turn to You.*

At this point, we have critically examined our lives and we have decided on our family mission. This week we will focus on systematic changes to our days to give ourselves freedom.

"In limits, there is freedom. Creativity thrives within structure."

- Julia Cameron

I am not, by nature, an orderly person. I'm actually pretty much the opposite. However, I have witnessed again and again the good it does my soul and mind when my house is in order. And so, I attempt to keep my home clean and uncluttered, plan meals, and stay ahead on work.

The most important 'tip' I can give you as a work at home mom is to routinize. Maybe you know that feeling that you are trying to juggle one hundred breakable plates, and if you so much as breathe it will all come crashing down. I've been there, and creating routines is a way to put down plates.

Routines do not mean a strict time schedule. They do mean that you have a game plan, and you generally stick to it. By writing down this plan, you take something off your mental load. You still have to grocery shop, or clean the bathroom, but you don't have to worry about when you'll get it done or what you need to buy.

I have routines for cleaning, cooking and meal planning, working, organizing the house, and more. We'll look at those areas soon. For today, let's just jot down the contents of some of those juggled plates. I think it can be eye opening to realize all that is happening inside our own brains, often subconsciously, until something starts to fall.

*Items in your mental load today:*

# Day 16

*Create in me a clean heart, O Lord.*

How can you routinize cleaning? I think this is perhaps the easiest to plan, although the execution can be difficult. Jot down a list of all the chores that need to be completed on a daily and/or weekly basis. Then assign each to a day/days and challenge yourself to complete those tasks each day. Add in monthly or seasonal tasks – each thing you plan for is another plate taken out of your mental juggling.

I'm including a basic outline of my family's cleaning schedule because I think it can be helpful to have a starting place.

### The Millers cleaning routine

*Daily:* Dishes after lunch and supper, pick up toys, sweep kitchen, make bed, load of laundry

*Monday: dust and clean bathrooms*

*Tuesday: vacuum*

*Wednesday: mop*

*Thursday: pick up bedrooms*

*Friday: vacuum and tidy kitchen*

I don't accomplish the scheduled tasks each day, but because of my routine, I quickly catch up and get back on schedule. The beauty of a routine (instead of a strict schedule) is that a routine is flexible and allows for the unexpected. If my toddler is sick, we might trade mopping for extra snuggles. At the same time, I don't see the stains on the kitchen floor everyday and keep on juggling that 'need to mop' plate. That plate is set down in the routine.

*What kind of routine might work for you for cleaning?*

# Day 17

*Give us this day our daily bread.*

Next up, let's create a plan for meals. I want you to create a plan that is going to work for your family, however I cannot overstate the difference that meal planning has made in my life. Not only do I not have to juggle the 'What will we eat tonight' plate, but I also (almost) always have the ingredients I need. Honestly, my adherence to meal planning began when I lived 25 minutes from the grocery store and running out for tomato paste in the afternoon was not a possibility. I now live within 5 minutes of several grocery stores, but with a toddler and naptime, grabbing ingredients at the last minute is still not feasible.

For my family, I have a list of approximately 30 different meals (complete with side options) that we all enjoy. I choose from the list, rotating chicken, beef, and fish/egg/vegetarian. I plan two weeks at a time and often look back about a month to repeat the plans. This gives us the freedom to plan around late work nights, social commitments, and weather (chili just really doesn't interest us once it warms up).

I write each meal on my daily planner, leaving days open for the leftovers I always make. Then, I compare the ingredients needed to what is in my pantry and write my shopping list. I sometimes use grocery pick-up services, especially in the summer when we have more fun places to be than pushing a cart through the store. We also typically eat leftovers or egg sandwiches for lunch so that I can focus on other things throughout the day.

I know other women who have luck planning a list of meals for the next week and having the freedom to choose from the list each day. There are excellent meal planning services out there as well. Try a system you think will work, and don't be afraid to tweak or rework the system so that it works for you and your family!

*Write your plan for feeding your family.*

# Day 18

*Lord, let my work give You glory.*

Working from home has its challenges. If you own your own business, it may be hard to separate yourself from your work or to put it down for family time. If you work set hours for an employer, you may struggle to entertain children or shuttle to children to childcare while completing quality work. We've already considered the benefits this work is bringing to you and your family. Today let's focus on routinizing your work as much as possible.

If you run your own business, consider which parts you can routinize. For instance, I struggled with social media content. Once I set myself a simple schedule (post Monday, Wednesday, and Friday) and a simple pattern (share an inspiration quote and then a photo), I was able to remove the 'social media posts' plate from my juggling. *Creativity thrives in structure!*

I have also worked to set up routines for creating inventory, fulfilling orders, and even setting goals for the future. Knowing that I have a set time to do these tasks keeps me from worrying all day about when I'll get the chance to do them.

I've found that these routines in my business have led to my setting bolder goals while fulfilling daily tasks without stress. For myself, I realized that accepting many custom orders leads to so much worry and struggle in my heart, so I limit custom orders. That may not work for your business; look for other ways to minimize the stress you deal with on a regular basis.

*What parts of your business cause the most stress or tax you the most mentally? What tasks do you find yourself falling behind on or forgetting? How can you create routines that give you the freedom to do what you love?*

# Day 19

*Lord, let my home encourage order in my heart.*

The final piece that you can routinize is organization. This may mean attempting minimalism – if you're interested, I highly recommend *Not of This World: A Catholic Guide to Minimalism* by Sterling Jaquith.

Organization can look different for different families, but I have a few ideas that might be useful:

- How can children be involved? Can they pick up their own toys? Unload the dishwasher? Sweep up? Depending on their age, they may be able to do much more!
- I know many parents who have great success with rotating tubs of toys. Children can focus on imaginative play easier without hundreds of options calling to them and clean up is less overwhelming with a single tub into which all the toys go.
- I firmly believe that everything in your home should have a 'place' – you know where it goes and that place makes sense given how and when the item is used. This makes organization a simple matter of matching items and their place, and not a challenging mental task.
- Consider a system for important paperwork – perhaps a couple file folders in a desk or a command center. Don't juggle plates if you don't have to!

*List ideas for organizing your home and, more importantly, for making organization simple and stress free.*

# Day 20

*Lord, direct my thoughts to you.*

Are you the queen of to-do lists? I started using a 'Bullet Journal' because I was always writing lists on scrap paper and then losing them and trying to remember what all was on that paper. One thing I've realized about a routinized life is that my to-do lists are much shorter. They tend to include only 'surprise' elements, such as needing to follow up on an important email or call a friend. My lists tend to be a 'brain dump' of the contents of all those plates I juggle. Now that I have routines for cleaning, cooking, working, and organizing, I have so many fewer plates up in the air.

As we complete this section on routines, I encourage you to look at your days and see if there are areas we haven't covered that could benefit from routines. For example, I haven't mentioned time with your husband, but my family does have a standing at-home date every Saturday night.

CAST YOURSELF INTO THE ARMS OF GOD AND BE VERY SURE THAT IF HE WANTS ANYTHING OF YOU, *He will fit you for the work and give you strength.*

—ST. PHILIP NERI

# Day 21

*Saint. Zita, help me to imitate you.*

Saint Zita is the patron saint of domestic servants, which seemed appropriate for us. She lived in Italy in the 13th century and worked as a servant for a wealthy family. She was very pious, but her fellow servants misinterpreted this as stupidity or hypocrisy. Zita would slip away to daily Mass or to a corner of the attic to pray. She would often be reprimanded, but God's angels would complete her work for her, so that she eventually won over the family for whom she worked.

When I read about Saint Zita, I am most reminded that if I give myself to God, he will not disappoint me. He cares deeply about the minutiae of my day, but He does not desire me to be lost in the details. When I feel that I am too busy to pray, Zita's example reminds that God will multiply the time I give him. Our God is a God of abundance, and he will not be outdone in generosity.

*How does Saint Zita's example inspire you in your work in the home?*

# Day 22

*Lord, keep me balanced, steady, and restful.*

The final week of this journey will bring together the areas we've discussed into a concrete path forward. We recognize the need for balance. Our work may be life-giving, an important mission, it may keep us sane. However, as a work-from-home mom, our work is not the ultimate goal. Becoming saints with our whole family is the goal.

As we think about balance, I would like to encourage you to look back at what you wrote on Day 3 – the list of good and joyful things in your life. What can you do to cultivate those things? What can you do to allow more time for the various parts of your life that are important to you? When you plan more attention and time to be given to the parts of your life that matter and that bring you joy, you will also begin to realize the parts of your life that are keeping you from you from joy.

In my family, I began to see that time to simply play with my son was life-giving to me and important to my child. I began to plan time each morning simply to freely play. Because I set aside that time, I was not frustrated that he was keeping me from fulfilling orders. That scheduled time fills us both up, so that we are ready to tackle the hard work of the day.

*As you consider the joys in your life, what needs more attention? What takes you away from that joy? Is there anything you can do minimize things that keep you from joy?*

# Day 23

*Lord, remind me to pray.*

I know from personal experience that prayer time can be one of the first areas to suffer from an overly busy life. Prayer requires quiet time, which may be in short supply. More than quiet, prayer requires entering a depth of ourselves that may feel overwhelming for a stressed-out mom. One of the great benefits of fighting for order in your life is that prayer time will become easier. Waking to a cleaner home, knowing your routine for the day, having meals planned – all of these things give you the mental ability to make time for prayer.

I encourage you to determine a routine for your prayer life. For myself, this is an area that needs work. I pray every morning before I do anything else. When I begin by offering my day, my work, my struggles to God, I see my heart ordered more rightly to God and His plans. I create Catholic products, and my work comes from a place of prayer, but as you could probably guess, sometimes business takes over. I get lost in financial or managerial tasks and lose sight of my ultimate goal (aka Heaven). I typically take a few minutes for prayer throughout the day, especially at meal times and a few minutes at the start of naptime. That may include spiritual reading, email devotionals, or just talking my Father. We pray a family Rosary each evening. I know many women pray and read Scripture while enjoying a hot cup of coffee in the morning. If you are mom to an infant, you likely have a different plan for prayer. I found that nursing sessions were a perfect time for a little prayer. The point is simply that it's vital to make time for quiet prayer. We cannot expect our relationship with God to grow or even be maintained if we never communicate with Him.

*What routine can you set up for prayer?*

# Day 24

*Lord, I thank you for the opportunity to work from my home and care for my children. I thank you for the talents and gifts with which You have blessed me and the opportunity to share them with my family and with the world. I beg you for your guidance as I endeavor to fulfill my multiple roles with grace and strength. Grant me the desire to do Your will and the discernment to understand Your will for me.*

*I ask for the intercession of all saints in Heaven who are mothers. Grant me the grace to guide my family to Heaven.*

*St. Gianna, pray for us*

*St. Monica, pray for us*

*St. Elizabeth Ann Seton, pray for us*

*St. Judith, pray for us*

*St. Zélie, pray for us*

*St. Zita, pray for us*

*Mary, Most Holy Mother of God, pray for us.*


Choose a special patron for your vocation of motherhood in this season of working from home. The women listed in the prayer above are understanding intercessors, or choose any Heavenly intercessor. Call upon that patron in times of joy and sorrow, laughter and frustration. Allow their prayers to sustain you.


*Who is the patron of your motherhood? Perhaps write a short 'morning offering' prayer to offer your day to God each morning.*

# Day 25

*Lord, grant me prudence in how I spend my time.*

We, as a society, talk a lot about 'having it all.' I don't believe that women (or men, for that matter) can have it all. There are choices to be made, and whenever when you choose one thing you are sacrificing something else. However, I do think women can be committed wives and mothers while working from home. In order to do this well, we must ensure that our time is spent on the areas most important to us.

Look back at your journaling from days 1 and 2. Are there problems remaining there that have not been addressed yet? For me, time spent on my phone has been an issue. For the longest time, I didn't have a smartphone...but let's just say I learned quickly. I love learning new things and the phone calls to me with its instant knowledge and 'connection' and information. However, I am slowly learning that the 'information' I learn from an hour on Facebook does me no good. I have gained true friendships and community from the internet, true, but I do not spend hours a day catching up with my family or my in-real-life friends. Why do I give my internet community so much time? This has been a difficult lesson for me, but I am committed to solving it. Perhaps one of the most useful solutions for me has been a monitoring app that locks my phone from most apps (I set it to allow texts, phone, camera, and the life-saving Maps app). I set my phone to lock up each evening, and my attention automatically returns to my family. (By the way, I recommend Quality Time for Android and Moment for iPhone.)

As I looked at my goals, I also saw that I did not have dedicated time for diving into work. Nap times and a few hours after bed are great, but at times I needed several hours to focus. My husband and I decided to switch off Saturdays. Every other Saturday, my husband is completely in charge of Benedict and the house, and I am free to come and go. I typically head to a local coffee shop and work for four hours, run errands, create products, and generally cross off most of my lingering to-do list. I come home refreshed in time for Vigil Mass and feel better able to deal with daily disruptions to my plans. I am currently writing this during a weekday while my son plays at a local nature school. We decided it made sense to pay for this school both for his experience, but also for additional work time for me.

*What can you do to address issues? What concrete plan of action can you draft? Pray for the strength to follow through.*

# Day 26

*Lord, grant me the grace to lavish attention on those right in front of me.*

In America, we hold a false idea that our work lives and our home lives are separate. Just a few generations ago, many families worked together farming or on a family business. That is not common today. For those of us blessed to work from home, the wisdom to integrate work and home life can be lacking. After all, we really have few models of this integration.

Working from home can mean that our work is always available. Every moment we have to make a choice. Someone who works in the office might decide to work late, but once they are home, work is left back in the office. Setting up a routine for when to put down work is crucial. Your children need your attention. Your house needs your attention. Your husband needs your attention. And prayer needs your attention.

Set up a plan for time when you will be 'at work' and time when you will be 'off'. For instance, I do not attempt to answer emails or fulfill orders in the first hour of the day. That is my time, for prayer, quiet, and sometimes creative work. As I mentioned, I set aside evening time for my family. I also do not answer emails after about nine at night – it can wait for the next day when I am refreshed and ready to go back to work.

An office worker who slaves at his desk fourteen hours a day is clearly a workaholic. So too, is the mother who feels compelled to reply to every email within moments, even though her children are begging her to read them a story. Set times when you are off work. I am in favor of my child seeing me work; he loves to 'help' me with orders. However, my goal is for him to grow up seeing the value of hard work. Not for him to grow up thinking that my work is more important than his needs and desires. This has meant making decisions to turn down opportunities in order to have less stress and more time for my family.

*When will you be 'at work?' When will you put down work? What can you do to signal the difference between the two? (Some suggestions: turn off the computer, put down the phone, step away from the sewing machine, etc)*

# Day 27

*Lord, fiat ordo.*

Throughout this journey, we have identified many changes that may help bring order to your life. Today, let's create a plan so that you know exactly what to implement going forward.

- Day 6 – what changes did you decide were needed? Have you begun to implement those changes?
- Day 13 – have you finalized your family mission statement? Is it on display in your home?
- Days 16-20 – have you implemented your new routines?
  - Cleaning
  - Cooking/meal planning
  - Working
  - Organizing
  - Additional needed routines
- Day 23 – have you implemented changes to your prayer life?
- Day 26 – have you decided on 'on' and 'off' hours?

I know firsthand that this process can be daunting. Change of any sort feels more difficult than continuing with the status quo. If you're still afraid to make a change, take a deep breath and go for it! Find five minutes when you normally scream into your pillow or eat chocolate in the closet, and implement one of the recommendations in this book. That investment will free up a little time to make the next change.

If you have been implementing changes throughout this journey, keep up the great work! You can feel proud that you are working toward a properly ordered life! Take the successes you've experienced so far and build upon them.

Are there tasks that are still taking up more than their fair share of mental load? Figure out a routine for them!

As babies are born, illnesses are dealt with, businesses are expanded, homeschool is begun or children go to school, your needs will change. Find the time to take this journey again any time you feel overwhelmed by life or feel that you are not giving your best to any of your roles. The specifics will change over time, but we pray always, "Fiat ordo."

*Are there additional changes you need to implement?*

# Day 28

*Saint Zélie, guide me in this journey.*

> "I have my two older girls with me, who are on vacation. It's a true pleasure for me, but also a real increase in work because I must take care of everything they'll need for the summer holidays. I'm having all their dresses repaired, so I am up to my neck in dressmakers. And in addition to this, I have urgent orders due this week; none are completed, and that worries me." (Letter 131, A Call to a Deeper Love)

If you've ever thought that saints have some 'extra' thing that you just don't have...read that quote again. Saint Zélie worried about all that she had to get done, both for her family and for her business. "A saint is a sinner who keeps trying," (attributed to Saint Josemaría Escrivá). We will fail in our attempts to keep order. Just in the weeks I've been writing this, I have failed. I've been overwhelmed and I've had to recalibrate and I've completely ignored my cleaning routine (you can tell, because, ants). But I'll keep trying and I know you will too. We'll stumble and we'll fall, but like Saint Zélie, we'll get back up.

> "Oh well, that's the day so far, and it's still only noon. If this continues I will be dead by this evening! You see, at the moment, life seems so heavy for me to bear, and I don't have the courage because everything looks black to me." (Letter 132)

Knowing that Saint Zélie faced many of the challenges I face gives me comfort. She remained ordered toward God, and I beg God for the grace to do so as well.

*What have you learned from this journey? Where do you still see disorder? What can you do to work toward order each day?*

# Conclusion

As you've probably noticed, I don't display myself as a 'hot mess mom.' I see value in acknowledging our struggles. Motherhood is difficult. Today, more than ever we are removed from the world of motherhood until our own child is brought forth. We have no rule book and few examples to look to. There is a connection to be had in sharing our failures and our stumbles. However, I personally make too many excuses for myself if I see myself as a 'hot mess mom.' My floors stay dirty, my hair stays in a ponytail, and, more importantly, I fail to challenge myself to improve. I see myself as a sinner who is trying. I probably fit the description of a hot mess mom often, but I am "made for greatness" (Pope Benedict XVI). I flee from the comfort of a worldly life and strive for greatness – to be a great mom, wife, Christian, and businesswoman.

If you prefer less structure or different routines than I have mentioned, please feel free to *go for it*. Comparison will steal the joy you feel in your own life. Your life does not need to look like my life or *anyone else's life*. I was discussing business lately with a fellow Catholic artisan, and I was struck by the difference in how we handle most aspects of our business. She thrives in custom work while I am overwhelmed by it. She is able to freely post whatever comes to mind on social media, while I am comfortable within a routine and structure. My point is, your life can be completely different from mine and we can both find order and draw closer to God.

I'd like to leave you will one final 'tip' – leave time for unexpected joys. As I've been writing this summer, a crew is working on our neighbors' driveways. I get shoes on and bags packed, only to be delayed as my son tries to inspect the concrete being poured. I am so thankful that my lifestyle allows us to spend ten minutes watching the trucks. He learns, he imagines, and he is so happy. There are days where we are hurrying to meet someone, and I don't have time for my son to sit in wonder. Believe me, the days of unhurried watching are much sweeter. Try your best not to be in a rush as often. That may mean leaving earlier. It may mean scheduling fewer activities. Our children learn from our example, and I want my son to learn that I have time for his interests and that his desires matter to me.

In fact, the entire idea of 'parenting' as we practice it did not exist until the 1970s! I almost found that impossible to believe, but it is true. When I feel pulled in a million directions and as if I need to decide now if I will homeschool my two-year-old through college, I take solace in this fact. There is no rule that I have to act this way. In fact, if I *do less* while *being more* for my son, I will be like most mothers throughout history. My generation was just about the only one so far to be 'parented,' and honestly? I'm not convinced it has all been for the best. Let your kids grow at their own pace, encourage them to be independent, and if they want to splash water and call it 'doing the dishes,' well, I think we should congratulate ourselves and tell them they make us proud.

We don't need to compare ourselves to *those moms* we see at the playground, drop-off line at school, or on social media. Because, newsflash, you are *not those moms*. You are you, God has entrusted these beautiful children and this beautiful work to *you*. Only you can fill this particular role! What a challenge and a shot in the arm at once!

I pray that this journey is helpful for you. I'd love to hear your thoughts at annunciationdesigns@gmail.com. The greatest compliment you could give me is to recommend this book to other women. I have poured my heart and soul into these pages, and I would be delighted to know that even one person benefitted from their contents.

Ad majorem Dei gloriam – to the greater glory of God!

**Acknowledgements:** *Dear Lord, I thank you for the inspiration, the desire, and the words. I pray that this book leads those who read it closer to Christ. Amen.* Thank you to my husband, who has encouraged me throughout this process and provided support in the forms of decaf coffee and entertaining of the toddler. Speaking of which, thanks to my son for teaching me what love is. Thank you to my editor, Anita Morin of FDS Creatives, who is a gem. Also, thank you to the best English teachers in the world, the late Ms. Bruns, Ms. Downy, the late Ms. Wourms, and Mr. Hemmert, who made it possible for this engineer/math teacher to decide to write books. God bless them and their insistence on my knowledge of metaphors, participles, and onomatopoeia.


**About the author:** Elayne Miller is a Catholic wife, mother, teacher, and artist. She is the hand-letterer behind Annunciation Designs, which offers products that call to mind the Sacred in the midst of the ordinary. She is passionate about helping her family and others lead intentional lives. Find links to follow, contact, and support her at annunciationdesigns.com

Made in the USA
Lexington, KY
12 August 2018